For my beloved Mary Augusta

THEE

THEE · A POEM BY CONRAD AIKEN
DRAWINGS BY LEONARD BASKIN

GEORGE BRAZILLER
NEW YORK

Books by Conrad Aiken
Collected Poems
Selected Poems
The Morning Song of Lord Zero
Collected Novels of Conrad Aiken
Collected Short Stories of Conrad Aiken
Collected Criticism of Conrad Aiken
Cats and Bats and Things with Wings
Mr. Arcularis: A Play

For information address the publisher:
George Braziller, Inc.
One Park Avenue
New York, N. Y. 10016

Library of Congress Catalog Card Number: 67–27521
Designed by Leonard Baskin
First printing
Printed in the United States of America

THEE

How to condemn THEE
yet also hymn THEE
how to praise THEE
yet also paraphrase THEE
how to proclaim THEE
yet also shame THEE

Wind blows
and mind blows with it
water flows
and mind flows with it
where shall I abide
cries the spirit
mind changes
and body changes with it
body changes
and mind changes with it
where shall I abide
cries the spirit
but also
says the spirit
north
south
east
west
at every compass point
I am still
I am at rest
I had and have no name
without it came
perhaps the wet
and still-by-night-dew-tightly-twisted
morning-glory

tiger at evening drinking
by moonlit water
and the all-thinking
skin of the earth
in which we move
and are a part
are single and same
all one hate
all one love.

Wind blows
but over what shall it blow
dead men encased in ice
men dying in snow
children lying in stretchers
their faces under the rain
the wounded animal
seeking out a hole
in which to lick his pain
and the bird
that symbol of the soul
coasting on the wind
for the last time
under the balsam
to hide his
death.
Cry death cry death
we come into the world
kicking and screaming
we go out of the world
kicking and screaming
and all between
is but

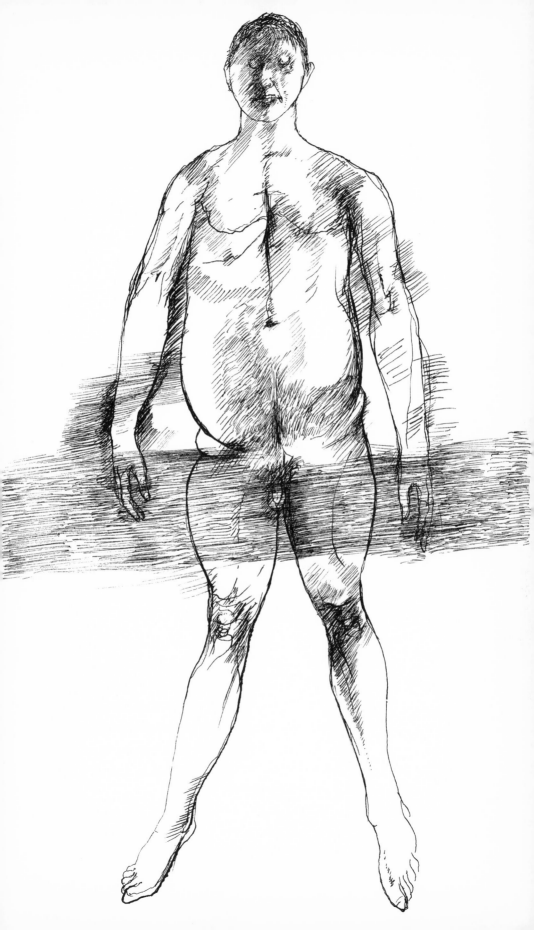

scheming
and
dreaming
and
seeming.

The spirit says
I am I
the spirit says
somewhere my cry
inarticulate and ignorant
though it be
may be heard
by the ultimate
unimaginable
THEE.
Who is that pitiless THEE
whom only in ourselves we see
or in the lightning-stroke
and stricken oak
and our young darlings doomed too soon to bed
without sin
and from within
by THEE and THINE?

Who is that hateful THEE
who makes a music of the sea
and of the clouds a harmony
or spreads a meadow broad and bright
with colors of delight
or brings the young with joy together
as birds of a feather
makes all the visible world a wedding feast
with love in every eye

and every breast
so that we think too long
that life is only song?
Unfaithful THEE
for suddenly the sea
rises and breaks the ship
blues every lip
cry death cry death
and we
and all the world we brought with us
thanks to THEE
go out of the world
or back to the world
to rejoin
unwillingly
and unconsciously
THEE.

Who is that splendid THEE
who makes a symphony
of the one word
be
admitting us to see
all things but THEE?
In the microcosm
in the macrocosm
it is THEE that we seek out
seeking to find
the workings of our mind
and THINE.
Wild columbine
admits THEE
wild rose
permits THEE

the seasons obey
THY reasons
yet further in our explorations do we go
the less we know.
Visible to the child
as butterfly
as lion
as mother
as father
moving under the microscope
or telescope
as smallest item or utmost star
yet THEE is still invisible
still indivisible.
How explain the morning that we wake to
the opening of the eye
the toothbrush
the toilet
the basket for soiled clothes
the fly's wing so designed
that it might be
a cathedral window
meant
for THEE?
Unkind THEE
did THEE have the fly in mind
and in THY warp and woof enwind
him and all his kind
to live his glorious dunghill day
then swept like snot away?

Who is that glorious THEE
sleeping and waking

the slow hushed life of tree
barely knowing
THINE own growing
then breaking and weeping
from THINE own sleeping?
We break and bud with THEE
put arms out like THY tree
and sing
inaudibly
in spring
as cold bark buds and breaks
and THEE awakes
and south wind shakes
the leaves that are THINE eyes
also THY breath
and
when THY calendar names it
death.

Nameless and shameless we
take THINE identity
to be
then
not to be
sharing with THEE
and daring
and O caring
for what is delicious
and what precious
learning how slowly what to choose
and what refuse

what use
and what abuse.
Laboriously the spirit learns
THY shadow upon us like the cloud's
shadow upon the meadow
as if perhaps in our slow growing
and the beginnings of our knowing
as if perhaps
O could this be
that we
be
THEE?
THEE still learning
or first learning
through us
to be
THY THEE?

Self-praise were then our praise of THEE
unless we say divinity
cries in us both as we draw breath
cry death cry death
and all our hate
we must abate
and THEE must with us meet and mate
give birth give suck be sick and die
and close the All-God-Giving-Eye
for the last time to sky.

Weather changes
and the spirit changes with it
climate changes
and the spirit changes with it
where shall I abide
cries the spirit
north

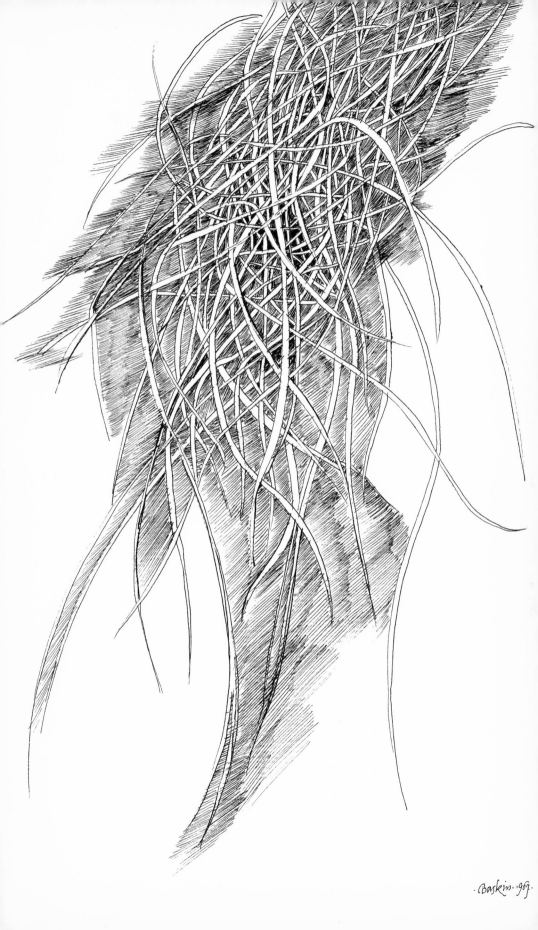

Baskin · 1967 ·

south
east
west
yet at no compass-point
is final rest
what fatal quest
is this
that we and THEE
in every THING
and every breast
must still pursue
and do?

Magnificent THEE
the syllables I speak
and which are THINE
and mine
still cannot equal THEE
who art becoming and have yet to be
and learn to speak
as we
with THEE.